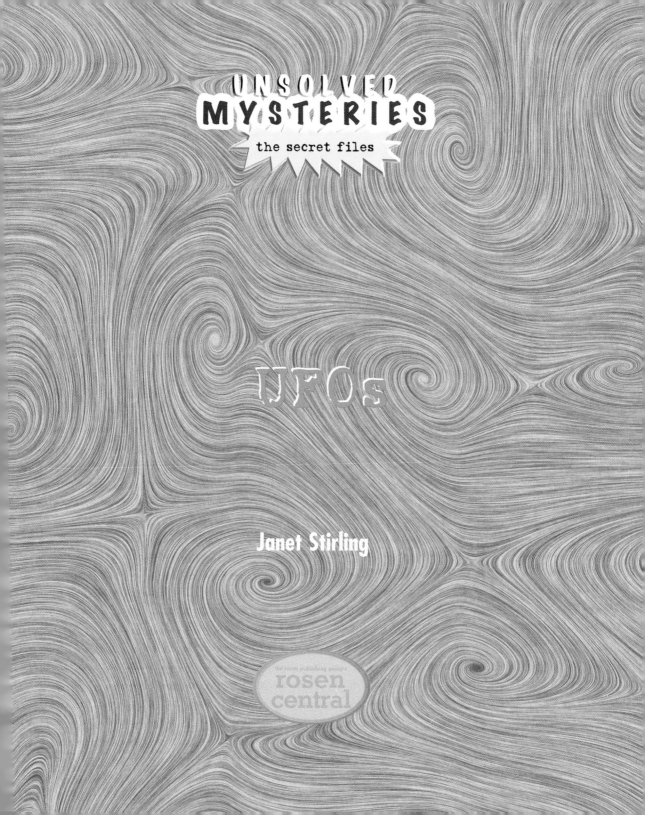

UNSOLVED MYSTERIES
the secret files

UFOs

Janet Stirling

the rosen publishing group's
rosen
central

To Josepha Sherman, a wonderful editor and a good friend

Published in 2002 by The Rosen Publishing Group, Inc.
29 East 21st Street, New York, NY 10010

First Edition

Library of Congress Cataloging-in-Publication Data

Stirling, Janet.
UFOs / by Janet Stirling.
p. cm. — (Unsolved mysteries)
Includes bibliographical references and index.
Summary: Examines case studies and reports of UFO encounters, discussing famous and lesser-known incidents, including Roswell and the case of the elk abduction.
ISBN 0-8239-3566-3 (library binding)
1. Unidentified flying objects—Juvenile literature. [1. Unidentified flying objects.]
I. Title. II. Unsolved mysteries (Rosen Publishing Group)
TL789.2 .S74 2001
001.942—dc21

2001004079

Manufactured in the United States of America

Contents

Although most UFO reports are later found to be misperceptions, optical or celestial phenomena, or outright hoaxes, a small percentage remain unexplained.

Introduction

The phrase "unidentified flying object" by itself isn't very exciting—until you consider what it means to most of us. When the average person hears someone say "UFO," he or she doesn't think of lost weather balloons or unusually high-flying eagles. What unidentified flying object means to the average person is spaceships, aliens, and the possibility that our planet is being watched by beings of higher intelligence, or at least more advanced technology.

Some people even think that UFOs are visitors from the far future or that they might be some species of unknown animal.

A good question to ask ourselves about these ideas might be: Are we jumping the gun here? Is all of this even possible? Or is there such a thing as being too skeptical?

We've gathered together some reports about UFOs that might help you make up your own mind.

1

Early UFO Sightings

How long have people been seeing strange things in the sky? Probably since there have been people to notice that something up there was different.

How long have people been assuming that those strange things were manufactured objects? At least since the late nineteenth century.

Between November 1896 and April 1897 there was a rash of sightings of a mysterious "airship" (which describes the most advanced flying technology of the time) whose origins, purpose, and crew were unknown. People described it as being a cylindrical gasbag with wings and propellers.

On April 19, 1897, the *Dallas Morning News* published a report of such an airship allegedly crashing in the town of Aurora in Wise County, Texas. According to the article, it collided with

Many of the early UFO sightings were of the first wave of aircraft, such as this airship designed and built for the Austrian military in 1909.

the tower of a windmill and exploded, scattering debris over several acres.

To quote the article, "The pilot of the ship is assumed to have been the only one aboard, and while his remains are badly disfigured, enough of the original has been picked up to show that he was not an inhabitant of this world." The article then goes on to give the time of the "pilot's" funeral.

This incident was forgotten until the late 1960s, when an article in the *Flying Saucer Review* attracted investigators to

Aurora. They found that no windmill had ever existed in the spot the article indicated and that there were no unmarked graves in the local cemetery.

In 1973, a United Press International news story claimed that elderly citizens of the town remembered the crash and had even collected "unidentified" metal from it. It also claimed that the UFO pilot's grave had been found through the use of a metal detector and that a "unique handmade headstone" was found on the spot. A court order was sought to exhume the "spaceman's" body.

Then, on July 4, 1973, the *Dallas Times Herald* carried the headline, "Grave Believed UFO Pilot's at Aurora, Entered, Robbed."

Once again investigation proved that things were not as they seemed. The hand-carved "tombstone" was a scarred rock, and the old-timers who had been interviewed all said they'd been misquoted and had never said they recalled the incident.

In the end, there was not one shred of evidence to back up the story of the Aurora crash.

Between 1909 and 1919, "airships" were seen over England. They were believed to be Germans, not aliens, scouting for an invasion. Reports of sightings also came in from mainland Europe,

Spectators watch the launch of the Barton Airship in 1905.

the United States, Canada, Japan, New Zealand, and South Africa, possibly the result of nervousness about World War I.

From 1909 until his death in 1932, Charles Fort, a well-known writer of strange occurrences, reported numerous incidents of "unknown, luminous things" seen in the sky, many of them disk-shaped.

Then, just before and during World War II, there were reports of ghost planes in the skies over Europe. Allied pilots often reported seeing what they dubbed "foo fighters" accompanying their flights. The objects were described as "large orange glows" or "small amber disks."

At first these were feared to be some Nazi secret weapon, but they appeared in the Pacific as well. None were reported to have directly interfered with Allied planes or crews; they simply flew quietly alongside them. After a while, less was heard of these objects, until they became an occasionally told UFO/ghost story.

After the war, beginning in May 1946, Sweden experienced sightings of spool-, torpedo-, or cigar-shaped rocketlike objects, often with small fins attached. At the time the fear was that German rocket technology was being used by the Soviets, and an extraterrestrial origin wasn't suspected. Between May and December of that year, 997 sightings were reported. Over 200 were of the "rocket-shaped" variety and were described as "metallic."

Soon other nations began to make reports of "ghost rockets." People in France, Denmark, Norway, Spain, Greece, Morocco, Portugal, and Turkey viewed flashing lights in their skies, sometimes accompanied by "an infernal roaring."

Eventually the Swedes were able to identify 80 percent of their sightings. The rest were listed as unidentified.

2

Some of the Classics

JUNE 24, 1947

On a summer afternoon, Kenneth Arnold, a successful businessman and private pilot, was flying home and intended to make a detour to Yakima, Washington, to help search for a missing plane that had crashed.

It was about three o'clock, he was flying at 9,200 feet, and the air was crystal clear—excellent flying weather. A flash of light off to his left caught his eye, and he looked toward Mount Rainier. He described what he saw as "a chain of nine peculiar looking aircraft flying from north to south at approximately 9,500 feet elevation and going, seemingly, in a definite direction of about 170 degrees." Arnold estimated that they were between twenty and twenty-five miles away.

They were flying at a high rate of speed and were bobbing and weaving slightly, which caused them to flash in the sunlight.

Captain Arnold *(center)* and two other pilots look at a photograph of the disk they claimed to have seen.

Arnold timed them as they passed Mount Rainier in the direction of Mount Adams. It took 102 seconds for the objects to pass between the two peaks. It is forty-seven miles between Mounts Rainier and Adams, which gave the objects a ground speed of 1,700 miles per hour. The speed of sound is approximately 740 mph, making the mysterious objects capable of flying at over twice the speed of sound! In 1947, no aircraft on Earth had that capability.

When Arnold later drew a picture of the crafts, he showed them having a flattened teardrop shape with a curved front surface, straight sides, and a back end with a rounded point. They were about fifty feet long, he thought, a bit less wide, but only three feet high. They had a mirror finish.

Arnold took his maps and calculations to the local FBI office but found it closed. He then went to the *East Oregonian* newspaper and spoke to an editor there. The report that went out on the Associated Press wire said, "Nine bright, saucer-like objects flying at 'incredible speed' at 10,000 feet altitude were reported here today."

Most researchers agree that this is the sighting that gave us the term "flying saucers."

CAPTAIN THOMAS F. MANTELL JR.

Captain Thomas Mantell was an experienced pilot. He flew with

the 165th Fighter Squadron of the Kentucky Air National Guard. He flew a propeller driven F-51 Mustang. The plane had a top speed of 437 mph and a ceiling of 41,900 feet, which could only be reached if the plane carried oxygen.

Captain Thomas Mantell Jr.

On January 7, 1948, none of the planes in Captain Mantell's squadron had oxygen because their mission was a low-altitude training flight.

At about 1:20 PM, the Kentucky State Police reported to Fort Knox that "an unusual aircraft or object . . . circular in appearance, approximately 250–300 feet in diameter" had been seen over Mansville, Kentucky. Fort Knox alerted Godman Airforce Base (AFB), which sighted the object at 1:45 PM. It looked roughly like a parachute with a red light at the bottom and was whiter than the clouds around it. It appeared to be either stationary or moving very slowly. Witness Private First Class Stanley Oliver said, "To me it had the resemblance of an ice-cream cone topped with red." It was much too large for any known balloon.

Civilians saw it, too, and reports came in from towns separated by as much as 175 miles. This means that the object must have been from 25 to 50 miles high. At that time, the United States had no plane that could fly so high.

At approximately 2:40 PM, Captain Mantell's group of four F-51s turned toward the object and began a spiral climb. At 2:45, Mantell reported, "The object is directly ahead of me and above me now, moving at about half my speed. It appears to be a metallic object, or possibly reflection of sun from a metallic object, and it is of tremendous size." At about 3:15, he reported, "I'm still climbing, the object is above and ahead of me moving at about my speed or faster. I'm trying to close in for a better look."

Somewhere between 15,000 and 22,000 feet, the other pilots turned back because of a lack of oxygen. Mantell told the tower that he would go to 25,000 for ten minutes. There followed a few garbled transmissions and then silence. Both radio and visual contact with Mantell had been lost. At 3:50 PM, the Godman tower lost sight of the object.

It was seen by others and described as "huge, fluid. It had a metallic sheen and looked like an upside-down ice-cream cone." At approximately 4:45 PM, an astronomer at Vanderbilt University watched an object in the sky southeast of Nashville, Tennessee, and described it as "a pear-shaped balloon with cables and a basket attached." Just before sunset, a number of airfield towers reported a flaming object in the midwestern sky, where it was visible for twenty minutes and then sank below the horizon.

A little after 5:00 PM, the shattered remains of Captain Mantell's F-51 were found on a farm in Franklin, Kentucky. The captain's watch had stopped at 3:18, probably the time when his plane struck the ground.

There have been a lot of dramatic stories about Captain Mantell—that his body was missing from the crashed plane, or that he bore strange wounds. According to records neither claim is true.

The simple truth appears to be that his curiosity got the better of him and he climbed so high that he blacked out from lack of oxygen, and his plane went into a spin and crashed.

The air force stated that Captain Mantell had been chasing a combination of the planet Venus and two balloons, and then closed the case.

In 1952, an investigator for Project Bluebook, the air force's famous study of UFOs, reopened the Mantell case. The investigator, Captain Edward J. Ruppelt, knew about the navy's high-altitude research, classified in 1948, that used huge Skyhook balloons. These balloons are 100 feet tall and 70 feet in diameter—as large as a small apartment building. He tried to discover a launch date that might have put one of the balloons in the vicinity of Mantell's flight.

But Captain Ruppelt could not verify that a Skyhook balloon had been released that day. As for Venus, while it had been seen in the daytime on that particular day, it could hardly be described as "enormous."

What could have distracted an experienced pilot to the extent that he ignored the dangers of oxygen deprivation and continued to pursue this UFO to his death?

SECOND LIEUTENANT GEORGE F. GORMAN

At around 9:00 PM on October 1, 1948, Second Lieutenant George F. Gorman of the North Dakota Air National Guard claimed to have an actual "dogfight" with a UFO.

He had remained in the air to do some night flying after the rest of his squadron had landed. The air was clear and there was no moon. His speed was 270 mph at an altitude of 1,500 feet. Below him he could see a Piper Cub airplane circling a football field. All was peaceful.

Then he noticed a blinking light moving swiftly from east to west. He contacted the air base's tower to see if there were other aircraft nearby. The answer was no. The pilot of the Piper Cub confirmed that he could see both Gorman's F-51 and the blinking light.

Meteorologists using a pilot balloon to test wind speed around 1935

Gorman sped off at full power to investigate. The object was traveling too fast to be caught by flying straight after it, so he turned in an attempt to cut it off. The light circled to the left, so Gorman circled to the right intending to confront it head-on. As it approached him, a collision seemed unavoidable, but the object veered off and passed over Gorman's plane.

"It was a ball of light, six to eight inches in diameter," he said later. "When it began flying at high speed the light increased in intensity and stopped flashing."

For a moment the lieutenant lost sight of the object, only to find that it had made a turn and was heading straight for him. Suddenly it began to climb. He pushed his F-51 after it, but at 14,000 feet his plane stalled out. He recovered and again began circling toward the light. It pulled away and again headed straight toward him. He managed to get above the object at 14,000 feet and went to full power, hoping to catch it as he dove. The light began to climb as though it would make another head-on pass, but instead it went vertical and continued to climb until it was out of sight.

Later Gorman said, "I am convinced that there was definite thought behind its maneuvers."

Gorman's F-51 was checked with a Geiger counter, and the reading showed measurably more radioactivity than nearby planes that hadn't been flown. Further investigation ruled out other aircraft or weather balloons in the area. This radioactivity seemed to be the first real evidence of an encounter with a flying saucer.

But by 1948 the case began to fall apart. The radioactivity was found to be typical for an aircraft flying at above 20,000 feet, where the thinner atmosphere offers less protection from cosmic rays that show up as increased radioactivity.

In fact, a lighted weather balloon was in the area at the time of the "dogfight." The fancy flying the light seemed to be performing was an illusion caused by its movement, Gorman's own enthusiastic flying, and the lack of a reference point in the night sky.

Furthermore, the witnesses in the Piper Cub didn't describe the light moving in the way Gorman said it did.

In 1949, Sidney Shalett, a writer with the *Saturday Evening Post*, located in Indiana, asked a pilot to make several passes at a weather balloon to see if it would appear to be a highly maneuverable, pilot-operated flying saucer.

Shalett reported, "He came down and told me, with some surprise, it definitely appeared to be turning at the same rate as his plane, and at times it even seemed to be turning faster than his aircraft." All of this would seem to completely discredit Second Lieutenant Gorman's experience.

Except Gorman had never claimed to fly to 20,000 feet, which then fails to explain the increased radioactivity detected on the plane.

LIEUTENANT FELIX MONCLA JR.

This case is also called the Kinross Disappearance after the air force base from which Lieutenant Felix Moncla's F-89 jet interceptor took off.

On November 23, 1953, Truax AFB in Wisconsin picked up a radar blip in a restricted airspace. As a precaution, Moncla and his radar officer R. R. Wilson were sent to investigate.

The object had been holding still, but suddenly it flashed off across Lake Superior while remaining visible on ground radar.

Lieutenant Moncla raced after the object at over 500 mph. After nine minutes, the F-89 began to gain slightly on the object. Ground radar operators watched as the jet closed in on the unidentified blip

A radar operator charts radar information aboard an aircraft carrier in the Pacific in August 1945.

until the blips suddenly seemed to merge into one.

The operators weren't alarmed at first because there was no way to tell how high either of the blips was flying. It was assumed that Moncla had flown over or under the UFO. But the single blip simply stayed there for a moment, then flashed off the screen.

All efforts to contact Moncla by radio failed. Search and rescue crews combed the area for hours aided by the Canadian Air Force. They found nothing: no trace of wreckage, no oil slick, no bodies.

The *Chicago Tribune* stated that the radar operator claimed the plane had hit something. The United States Air Force quickly denied this. After suggesting that the F-89 might have hit a Canadian DC-3 or an RCAF jet, the Canadian Air Force denied that any of its aircraft were over the lake during the chase.

It's possible that the F-89 dropped into the lake without breaking up, in which case the usual signs of a crash wouldn't be apparent. That doesn't explain why radio contact ceased, or why Moncla and Wilson didn't eject. And there have been numerous reports of radio transmissions being interfered with and automobile engines being stopped by UFOs.

Shortly after this incident, two fighter pilots reported that they were being followed by a UFO. Before signaling the base, they went through a series of maneuvers to make sure they weren't seeing a reflection on their canopies or perhaps an unusually bright planet. But the large, bright object stayed in the same position and continued following them. After what had happened to Moncla, they were understandably reluctant to turn in pursuit. Finally, as they neared the base, the pilots decided to make their move and turned toward the UFO.

For a split second it continued to follow, then flashed off at high speed. In both cases, the pursued object was never satisfactorily identified.

3
UFO Landings and Crashes

The first UFO we'll look at was detected by radar over the Oneida, New York, area in 1962, heading west at a high altitude. As the object moved into the Midwest, the Air Defense Command began alerting bases to watch for it. In Phoenix, Arizona, interceptors were scrambled to seek it out.

In Utah, witnesses who saw the bright, oval-shaped, red-orange object flash overhead claimed to hear a sound like jet engines. This is unusual, because UFOs are mostly described as soundless or emitting a slight whine. The UFO was sighted near Eureka, Utah, where it touched down briefly. It was thought to have interrupted electrical service from a nearby power station. A few minutes later it was seen heading west again. Suddenly, seventy miles northeast of Las Vegas, the object disappeared from radar screens at a time and place that coincided with reports of a blinding midair explosion.

On April 19, the *Las Vegas Sun* ran a headline stating, "Brilliant Red Explosion Flares in Las Vegas Sky." The roar of the explosion was heard for miles, and the flash of light was so brilliant that it lit up the town of Reno like the noonday sun. Police searched the desert for wreckage but found nothing.

Project Bluebook listed it as a radar case, confirming that it had been traced by radar. However, the report stated that there was insufficient information for a scientific analysis. The sighting in Eureka had been a meteor, it said. But meteors can't be tracked by radar, and they don't take off again once they've landed. As for the exploding object near Las Vegas, the air force wouldn't label it a meteor and there were no reports of missing aircraft.

El Indio, Mexico

In December 1950, a woman visiting a dude ranch in Texas wrote to her husband about a most unusual incident. She and the other guests and ranch workers had observed what seemed to be an airplane in distress flying overhead. They thought it might have come down over the Mexican-American border. The next day several of the ranch cowboys rode out to see if they could find something.

They found wreckage, but it didn't look like any airplane they'd ever seen. There were bodies strewn about, badly burned. The

UFO crashes in remote places are almost impossible to prove.

cowboys said it looked as though the craft had been piloted by children. The next day they returned to find the area swarming with Mexican and American officials and military personnel arguing over jurisdiction. No one could agree if the crash remains came from north or south of the border. The cowboys were chased off before they could get too close. The incident was described in a briefing paper for President Dwight Eisenhower. Nothing more is known about it.

UBATUBA, BRAZIL

In September 1957, several Brazilian fishermen claimed they had seen a flying disk. It came toward them at a very high speed, dived at them, turned in a tight circle, and began a rapid climb. Seconds later it exploded, showering the beach at Ubatuba with fragments. The men wrote to the local newspaper and included several of the fragments with their letter.

When Dr. Olavo Fontes, the Brazilian representative for the Aerial Phenomena Research Organization (APRO), first read the story, he thought it must be a hoax. But he had the samples of the metal examined by a local chemist. The chemist concluded that it wasn't from a meteorite because it was too light. Many meteors are composed of nickel and iron, two heavy metals. But the samples were a lighter metal that showed signs of having been burned. Spectroscopic analysis revealed that the sample was magnesium and of a purity unobtainable in nature. Dr. Fontes sent a report and the samples to APRO headquarters in the United States.

APRO sent a small piece of the metal to the air force for analysis. Unfortunately, their spectrograph operator destroyed the sample without getting an exposed plate. It may have been carelessness or a malfunction, but the destruction of the sample isn't necessarily proof of malice on the part of the air force.

APRO then sent a sample to the Atomic Energy Commission, which found that the sample was slightly denser than normal. Lab

This 4.5-billion-year-old rock, found in Antarctica in 1984, is believed to have come from Mars.

results also showed that the metal probably came from something that had broken apart rapidly, as in an explosion.

Subsequent analysis by Dr. R. S. Busk of the Condon, Colorado, UFO Study revealed a high content of strontium, a soft, silver-white element. The study also said that magnesium of the same purity was created at Dow Laboratories.

It was also found that the Ubatuba samples had better high-temperature properties than samples of the Dow Labs metal. Therefore, although Dow had magnesium of equal purity, it could not have produced the samples from Brazil.

How something only available in an American laboratory came to be found on a beach in Brazil was not something the Condon, Colorado, UFO Study commented on.

ROSWELL, NEW MEXICO

The incident in Roswell has to be the most famous UFO crash ever. Many books have been written about it, so we'll give just the basic story.

On July 2, 1947, many people in Roswell reported a large, disk-shaped object flashing by overhead and showing signs of instability in its flight. An explosion was heard, but because there was a thunderstorm in progress, no particular attention was paid to the burst of sound. The next morning, objects that were described as everything from scattered debris to "a crashed airplane without wings" or "narrow wings" and "a fat fuselage" were found.

Rancher William "Mac" Brazel found debris scattered over an area nearly a mile long and half a mile wide. He collected some of it and stored it in his barn. Brazel called the sheriff when he heard about the UFO sighting, and soon news about the debris made its way to Major Jesse Marcel at the Roswell Army Air Field. Marcel visited

Air force officers examine and identify a "weather balloon" found near Roswell.

Brazel's place and collected some samples. Upon Marcel's return to the base, Colonel William Blanchard ordered Lieutenant William Haut to release a statement to the media that the wreckage of a flying disk had been recovered. Almost immediately, Blanchard's commanders ordered that the story be retracted.

According to Marcel, the samples he recovered included a metal that couldn't be burned but was as light as balsa wood. Some of them appeared to be struts or beams that had hieroglyphic-like writing on them. Hammering on the metal with a hammer produced no dents. There was also a type of foil-like metal that could be crumpled into a ball and then would straighten itself out.

As well known as the Roswell crash is for the unique properties of the debris, it's better known for the five alien bodies allegedly found at the site. The bodies were clothed in flight suits without visible fasteners. Each was five feet tall or less, thin and pale, with a head slightly larger than a human's would be, and completely hairless. The aliens' eyes were only slightly larger than those of normal humans and had pupils. Their noses were small but defined, and their mouths were lipless. Their hands had four long, thin fingers. Immediately after the crash, the debris and alleged bodies were taken by the army air force (as it was known in 1947) and never seen again.

The most recent press release from the air force regarding the Roswell incident claims that a balloon research project code-named MOGUL crashed in the area. The bodies, it explained, were test dummies taken aloft for scientific testing. The army air force units that gathered the material were simply on-site for a normal retrieval.

The air force claimed that a number of different incidents, often separated by years, "have been consolidated and represented to have taken place in two or three days in July 1947."

This may be true, but air force test dummies, while hairless, have very prominent noses and lips and look much more like puppets than anything that might once have been alive.

4

Astronaut Sightings

Several times during flights, astronauts have seen objects that couldn't be identified. NASA (National Aeronautics and Space Administration) generally knows what's orbiting Earth by keeping track of satellites and space debris such as discarded booster rockets. So when an astronaut asks about something seen, NASA can usually give a straight answer. But not always.

Astronaut Jim McDivitt on Gemini IV in 1965 spied a silvery-white cylindrical object with arms or antennae projecting from it. It appeared to be moving toward him when suddenly it disappeared.

During an air-to-ground transmission, McDivitt was asked, "You still looking at that thing up there?"

The astronaut answered, "No, I've lost it . . . I only had it for just a minute. I got a couple of pictures . . . but I was in free drift, and before I could get the control back I drifted and lost it."

On the third day of Gemini V, an eight-day mission flown by LeRoy Gordon Cooper and Charles Conrad in August 1965, Flight

The Gemini V flight crew pose in their space suits with a model of the spacecraft.

Director D. Christopher Kraft asked, "Hey, do you guys have anything flying alongside of you?"

The astronauts replied, "Negative. Why did you ask?"

"We have a radar image of a space object going right along with you from 2,000 to 10,000 yards away," Kraft said. "Their radar return is approximately the same magnitude as Gemini V."

Cooper and Conrad still denied seeing anything.

In the control log is the following statement: "A tumbling radar signature was observed. This info is to be withheld pending further investigation."

Cape Canaveral continued to track the UFO until Gemini V dropped below the curve of the earth. When Gemini V reached the next tracking station in Carnarvon, Australia, the UFO was gone.

In 1965, Gemini VII astronauts Frank Borman and James Lowell contacted NASA in Houston to say they had "a bogey at twelve o'clock high." Ground control thought at first that it was the booster from their own rocket, but the astronauts said that they had that in sight at the same time as they were watching the UFO. It slowly tumbled out of sight and still remains unidentified.

Michael Collins and John W. Young flew the Gemini X mission in 1966. They both observed five objects in orbit together. These objects, too, remain unidentified.

On their way to the first Moon landing in 1969, the Apollo XI crew—Buzz Aldrin, Neil Armstrong, and Michael Collins—were one day out when they saw something strange. Thinking they were looking at their own Saturn IV booster rocket, they called Houston for confirmation only to be told the booster was 6,000 miles away.

The UFO seemed to the astronauts to be of "a sizeable dimension," and appeared brighter than other objects going by. Armstrong said during the mission debriefing, "We should say it

Command post of the North American Air Defense at the Peterson Air Force Base, Colorado

was right at the limit of the resolution of the eye. It was very difficult to tell just what shape it was. And there was no way to tell the size without knowing the range [distance from the Apollo XI] or the range without knowing the size."

At one angle, the object had a shape something like "an open suitcase." When looked at through an off-focus sextant, it appeared to be a "hollow cylinder" or "two rings." When they changed the focus on the sextant, the cylinder was replaced by "this open book shape." The object remains unidentified.

The crew of Skylab II in 1973 also sighted something mysterious. It seemed to be a large, star-shaped object, but brighter than a planet or a star. The crew watched it slowly rotate for about ten minutes, estimating that it was between thirty and fifty nautical miles from Skylab. Despite the best efforts of NASA and the North American Air Defense Command, it, too, remains unidentified.

5

The Recent Files

There seem to be fewer reports these days of UFOs, but by no means are UFOs finished with us.

MARCH 19, 1992

It was 3:50 AM when Luis Delgado, a patrolman for the Haines City, Florida, police department, caught sight of a green light in his rearview mirror. As he drove, the light seemed to be pacing his cruiser. He slowed down, and the object flew over the cruiser with a brilliant green glow. Alarmed, he pulled to a stop and the cruiser's power died, leaving him without a radio.

Delgado stepped out of the car and watched the glowing, fifteen-foot-wide object silently hovering about ten feet off the ground in front of him. It cooled the warm night air enough to form a mist around it. Then, after several minutes, it suddenly sped away.

The young officer returned to his cruiser and found the electrical system working again.

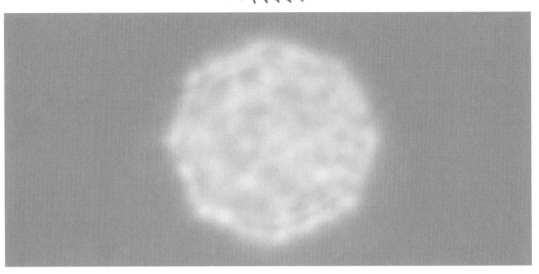

Telephoto view of an unidentified object seen flying over Mexico City on July 12, 2000.

Many times when people out driving see a UFO they report that their cars mysteriously stopped. Those with CB radios report that their radios wouldn't work either. That makes the above story something of a classic.

SEPTEMBER 27, 2000

Four friends had gathered in the wilds of central Idaho for their annual hunt, like they'd been doing for over twenty years, when they saw something very strange.

It was almost 10:00 PM when one of them left their camper to get some food from his pickup truck. He suddenly felt strange, "like a thick blanket was suspended overhead." As he stepped up on the rear tire of his truck to reach the food, his flashlight beam swung upward and illuminated something directly above him. Glancing up, he was so startled that he fell from the truck to his knees in shock.

Silent and dark, the object hung motionless over their campsite. It was triangular in shape and had rounded corners, and the man's first impression was that it was as large as a football field: stretching above him hundreds of feet on each side and blotting out the sky above him.

He shouted for his friends. Meanwhile, dim, circular white lights lit at the three corners of the object, and a large, prominent red light in the center of the craft began to blink rapidly. The object began to emit a whining sound.

Two of the campers came out in time to witness the object moving away toward a nearby mountain. They had the object in sight for almost a minute as it maneuvered up a narrow canyon in the side of the mountain. They described its motion as "like a hockey puck gliding over ice," very smooth and unwavering.

Two of the men were so unnerved that they spent the rest of the night in a motel. The men who stayed behind reported that the next morning two jet fighters flew down the same valley the object had flown up the night before, passing directly over their camp. The jets didn't move through the canyon as smoothly as the mysterious object.

FEBRUARY 25, 1999

In the mountains of Washington State, fourteen forestry workers were planting seedling trees when three of them noticed a small, disk-shaped object drifting over a nearby ridge. At first the three thought it might be a parachute, but they quickly realized that it wasn't. It silently descended into a valley north of them with a slight "wobble" to its flight, traveling toward a herd of elk. It succeeded in getting quite close to the animals before the elk bolted. Most of them ran up a slope to the east.

One adult elk, however, trotted north. The object quickly moved directly above the lone elk and lifted it off the ground, though the watching men couldn't see how this was done.

The object seemed to wobble more. As it rose higher, the elk that was suspended below the disk rotated slowly beneath it and seemed to be pulled closer to it. The witnesses said that the object seemed to grow slightly after it had picked up the animal.

If You See a UFO

What should you do if you see a UFO?
The same thing you should do if you witness an accident.

1. First, remain calm. If you get too excited, you might forget important details.

2. Notice things. Note the time when you first see the object. When it disappears, make note of what time the sighting ends. Establish what direction the object came from and where it went. Were there airplanes in the sky at the same time? If so, where were they in relation to the object and what were they doing (for example, were they chasing it)?

3. If you have a camera, take pictures. If at all possible try to include something that will give an idea of the object's size, such as a tree or telephone pole.

4. As soon as possible write down what you have seen. This is where your attention to details, such as the time and the direction of the object's flight, will come in handy. Make a diagram of the flight path, including any zigzagging it made. Make a drawing of the object itself.

5. If you are with others when the sighting occurs, do not discuss what you've seen until everyone has written about it and made his or her own drawings. Witnesses almost always see things differently, and when they discuss the event they may change each other's memory of what they've witnessed.

6. If the UFO has left physical evidence, such as pieces of metal or even footprints, do not touch them. Leave them as they are, perhaps placing a marker beside the evidence to make it easier to find again.

7. **VERY IMPORTANT.** Do not approach the UFO if it should land or come close to the earth. There have been reports of people suffering burns or developing strange, warty growths over their exposed skin. So don't take chances.

8. Report the sighting as soon as possible. Contact one of the following:
   UFO Reporting and Information Service (206) 721-5035
   Mutual UFO Network (830) 379-2166
   National UFO Reporting Center (206) 722-3000

With the elk below it, the object slowly ascended the slope toward some trees. It seemed to brush the tops of the trees and then reverse its course. Making a 360-degree turn, which resulted in greater altitude, it headed toward the trees once more, moving more quickly and at a steeper angle.

As it climbed higher, the men could no longer see the elk and they assumed that it must have been brought into the craft, although they hadn't seen any sort of door through which it might have entered. The object continued to ascend and simply disappeared from sight.

Afterward, the witnesses said, the herd of elk remained in the general area, but more closely huddled together than they had been. One of the witnesses added, "And so were we."

Glossary

briefing paper A short statement or summary of important facts.

CB Citizens band radio.

ceiling The maximum altitude that a given aircraft can reach.

debriefing The asking of questions about a completed mission or undertaking.

debris Scattered fragments, especially of wreckage.

diagram A drawing meant to represent an object or area showing the relation between parts or places.

disk A flat, thin circular object.

dogfight Close combat between fighter aircraft.

extraterrestrial Outside the earth or its atmosphere; an alien being.

gasbag Basically a balloon, something made to hold lighter-than-air gas.

hieroglyphics Words written in the form of pictures instead of letters.

interceptors Small jet aircraft designed to catch and fight other planes.

magnitude A thing's size or extent. In astronomy, refers to the relative brightness of a star, ranging from a rating of one for the brightest to six for those just visible to the naked eye.

maneuverable Capable of quick and light or skillful movement.

mph Miles per hour, the number of miles that can be traveled in an hour.

nautical miles A unit of approximately 2,025 yards (1,852 meters).

Nazi German National Socialist Party. Part of the Axis powers, which was the union of Germany, Italy, and Japan during World War II.

Piper Cub A small, light, propeller-driven aircraft, often having only one engine.

reference point A fixed place from which position and distance are reckoned.

rotating When something is turning, or being caused to turn, on its axis or center.

Soviets People of the former United Soviet Socialist Republic, also known as the Soviet Union. Once considered to be the same thing as "Russians."

spectrograph An apparatus for photographing the spectrum.

spectrographic analysis A spectrum is like a fingerprint, in that every material produces a unique spectrum. Spectral analysis provides information about an object's chemical composition.

squadron A unit of ten to eighteen aircraft.

strobe Intense, very brief flashes of light.

tower The control tower; a tall building at an airport from which air traffic is controlled.

transport A ship or aircraft used to carry soldiers or supplies.

For More Information

Mutual UFO Network (MUFON)
103 Oldtowne Road
Seguin, TX 78155-4099
(830) 379-9216
(800) 836-2166
Web site: http://www.rutgers.edu/~mcgrew/mufon/index.html

National UFO Reporting Center (NUFORC)
P.O. Box 45623
University Station
Seattle, WA 98145
(206) 722-3000
Web site: http://www.ufocenter.com

UFO Reporting and Information Service
P.O. Box 832
Mercer Island, WA 98040
(206) 721-5035
Web site: http://www.tje.net/para/organizations/uforis.htm

CANADA

Canadian UFO Research Network
592 Sheppard Avenue West
Downsview, ON M3H 6A7
(416) 787-1905

For Further Reading

Corso, Philip J., and William J. Birnes. *The Day After Roswell.* New York: Pocket Books, 1997.

Herbst, Judith. *The Mystery of UFOs.* New York: Aladdin Paperbacks, 1997.

Hynek, J. Allen. *The UFO Experience: A Scientific Enquiry.* New York: Marlowe and Co., 1999.

Peebles, Curtis. *Watch the Skies! A Chronicle of the Flying Saucer Myth.* New York: Berkeley Publishing, 1995.

Picknett, Lynn. *The Mammoth Book of UFOs.* New York: Carrol & Graf, 2001.

Randle, Kevin D. *The Roswell Encyclopedia.* New York: Avon Books, 2000.

Randle, Kevin D., and Donald R. Schmitt. *The Truth About the UFO Crash at Roswell.* New York: M. Evans and Co., 1994.

Index

ABOUT THE AUTHOR

Janet Stirling lives in Santa Fe, New Mexico, with her husband, science fiction writer S. M. Stirling, and their cat, Nyla.

PHOTO CREDITS

Cover, p. 4 © Digital Art/Corbis; p. 7 © National Aviation Museum/Corbis; pp. 9, 19 © Hulton-Deutsch Collection/Corbis; pp. 13, 23, 31, 34 © Bettmann/Corbis; p. 14 © Center for UFO Studies; p. 27 © Stan Wayman/TimePix; p. 29 © NASA/TimePix; p. 36 © Corbis; p. 38 © Reuters New Media Inc./Corbis.

SERIES DESIGN AND LAYOUT

Geri Giordano